A woman NEEDS A MAN LIKE A DOG NEEDS A TUTU

ROVER

Daisy Hay

summersdale

A WOMAN NEEDS A MAN LIKE A DOG NEEDS A TUTU

Summersdale Publishers Ltd
46 West Street
Chichester
West Sussex
PO19 1RP
UK

www.summersdale.com

Printed and bound in China

ISBN: 978-1-84953-099-6

Substantial discounts on bulk quantities of Summersdale books are available to corporations, professional associations and other organisations. For details contact Summersdale Publishers by telephone: +44 (0) 1243 771107, fax: +44 (0) 1243 786300 or email: nicky@summersdale.com.

Contents

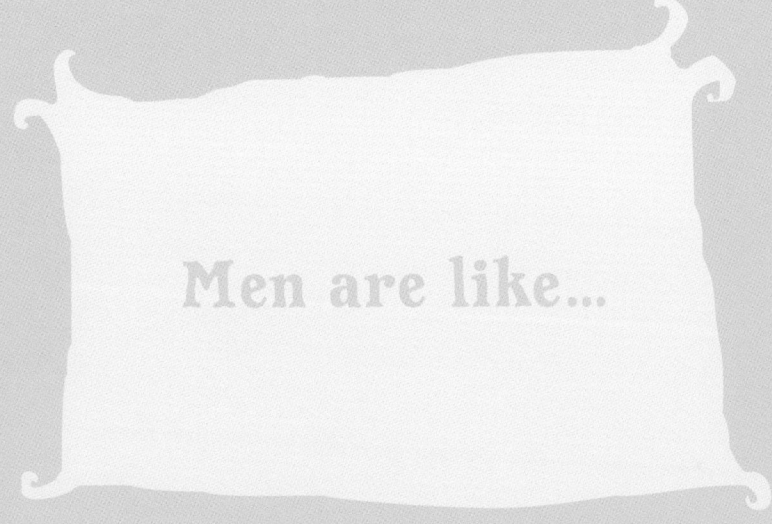

Men are like...

... beer bottles

- empty from the neck up!

... adverts

– entertaining and enticing, but
you can't believe a word they say.

... bike helmets

– useful in an emergency,
but a bit silly looking.

... the weather

- you can't do anything to change them, but you can't seem to stop talking about them either.

... **roller coasters**

\- **exhilarating at first but they can leave you feeling a little unbalanced.**

... computers

- it's always best to have a backup.

... fires

– dangerous if left unattended.

... chocolate

- sweet, smooth and head
straight to your hips.

... Swiss cheese

- they smell of sweaty socks
and take way too long to mature.

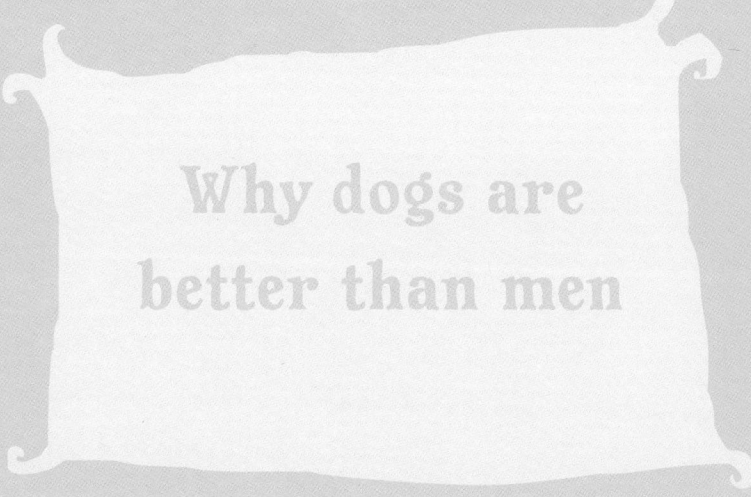

Why dogs are
better than men

In some ways, men and
dogs are very alike

- they'll both shed hair all over your sofa...

...and when they want something they'll give you those gooey, puppy-dog eyes.

But there the similarities end.

A dog can be housetrained...

... and it really does like to go
for long walks on the beach.

Dogs don't go bald in their senior years...

... or have a mid-life crisis and get a tattoo and start wearing tight leather trousers...

... and they won't trade you in for a younger model because you've regained a bit of 'puppy' fat.

Dogs won't laugh at you for 'throwing like a girl' when you're playing fetch.

It's true that dogs aren't perfect...

... like men, they might snore or
make unpleasant smells...

... but you can turf them out when they do,
and they'll still love you in the morning.

A dog will accept unquestioningly who's boss...

... they know when they've
done something wrong...

... and they have no qualms about
grovelling to win back your affections.

You will never find yourself in a nightclub eyeing up other dogs...

.... or wishing your dog could dance like they do.

But best of all, you will never look at your dog and wonder if you still love it

- or if it still loves you.

What a man says
and what he
really means

Hi, nice to meet you!

= You female, me male. We mate now?

It's a long story.

= You're never going to sleep
with me again if I tell you this.

I think we should just be friends.

= I'm not into you, but I'm hoping you'll set me up with your hot mate.

Yeah, I totally agree.

= I have no idea what you just said
- I am mesmerised by your breasts.

We're not lost. I know precisely where we are.

= We're never going to be seen alive again.

Why don't you stop doing the housework and relax for a while?

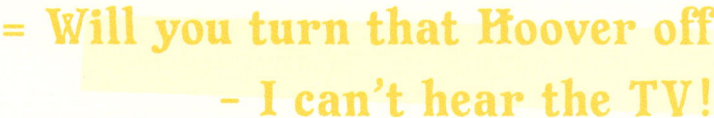

= Will you turn that Hoover off
– I can't hear the TV!

Of course I'm listening to you – I'm just tired.

= That blonde at the next table is really fit!

That's interesting, dear.

= Oh God, is she still talking?

I'm feeling pretty rotten.
You go on out and have fun without me.

= I've got man flu and it's almost certainly
fatal. I'll never forgive you if you
leave me alone to die here!!!

Can I walk you home? I'd just
feel better knowing that
you got home safely.

= So, shall we go back to your
place for some casual sex?

I'm just popping out for
a swift half, love.

= When you next see me, I will be clutching a
half-eaten kebab and mumbling incoherently
about how I 'bloody love you'.

We don't need material things to prove our love for each other.

= I forgot our anniversary again.

That's not what I meant.

= That's exactly what I meant, I just hadn't intended for you to hear it.

Will you marry me?

= Can I move in to yours? My housemates are filthy, I can't work the washing machine and the fridge is always empty.

Explain the offside rule? There's no point – you'll never get it.

= I've no idea how it works either but I don't want to look stupid in front of my mates.

Men: your
questions answered

What can do the work of five men?

A woman.

What's the difference between a man and a shopping trolley?

Sometimes, a shopping trolley can have a mind of its own.

How do you get a man to climb onto your roof?

Tell him the drinks are on the house.

What's the difference between an ugly man and an attractive one?

About four glasses of wine.

What should you do if your man walks out on you?

Close the door before he changes his mind.

Why do men keep empty milk bottles in their fridges?

In case anyone asks for black coffee.

How does a man demonstrate that
he is planning for the future?

He buys fifteen cases of beer.

How many men does it take to change a toilet roll?

Nobody knows – it's never been done.

What is a bachelor?

A man who has missed his chance to make some poor woman miserable.

Why a dog needs
you more
than a tutu

Every dog needs a shampoo once in a while...

... not even they can get away with cute *and* smelly.

Come rain or shine, all dogs
need to be taken for walks...

... even if they're not easily led.

Without you, your dog would have no one to enjoy fetching sticks, newspapers, slippers and all manner of things for...

... it's just fetching that first cup of tea in the morning that's a bit tricky.

Your dog may still look good
after a late night with the boys...

... but not as good as when it's
walking down the street with you.

Your dog can fart shamelessly
when you're around...

... and it doesn't mind when you do it too!

They need you to ferry them everywhere... to the park... to the woods...

... but at least they don't criticise your driving.

Your dog needs you to deal with its business...

... and maintain its Facebook profile.

So, you think the dog that has everything needs a ballet outfit?

That would be tutu much.

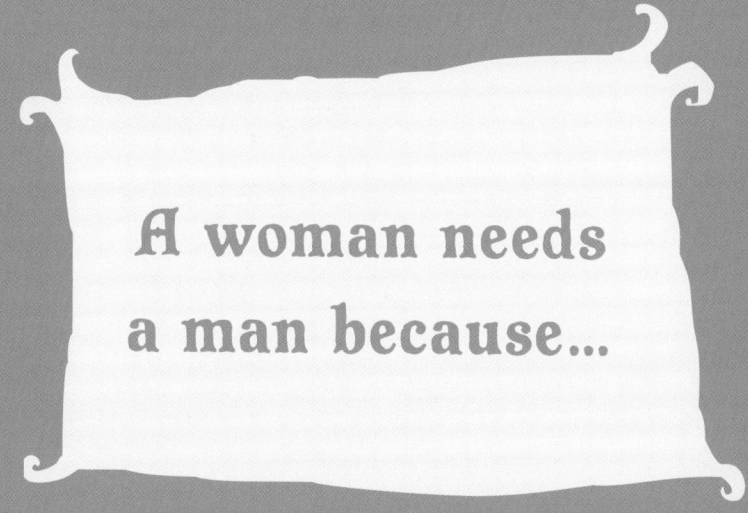

A woman needs
a man because...

... cars don't fill themselves.

... at family get-togethers, it's good to have someone to palm off on Aunt Myrtle.

... though you could put up that set of shelves yourself if you really tried, men seem to enjoy that sort of thing so much more.

... you can tap into their supply of razors when yours run out.

... they always travel light, so you can use their baggage allowance for those extra pairs of shoes when you go on holiday.

... they're handy for those few sporting questions that come up when you're playing along to *Who Wants to be a Millionaire?* on the TV.

... there's always someone to hold your handbag while you hit the dance floor for some serious boogying.

... sometimes you need someone to tell you that 'no, your bum doesn't look big in that' – even if you know that secretly they didn't even bother to look before saying it.

And remember...

A man is good for at least one thing - for
letting your beloved pooch out in the morning!

Have you enjoyed this book?
If so, why not write a review on your favourite website?

Thanks very much for buying this Summersdale book.

www.summersdale.com